<u>F</u> -AVOR

<u>A</u> -UTHORITY

<u>I</u>- NSPIRATION

<u>T</u> -REASURE

<u>H</u> -OPE

MARCIA S. WATSON

authorHOUSE®

AuthorHouse™
1663 Liberty Drive, Suite 200
Bloomington, IN 47403
www.authorhouse.com
Phone: 1-800-839-8640

First published by AuthorHouse 11/8/2007

ISBN: 978-1-4343-4302-4 (sc)

Printed in the United States of America
Bloomington, Indiana

This book is printed on acid-free paper.

...therefore the Lord establish the kingdom in his hands.... 2 Chronicles 17:5

DEDICATION

This book is dedicated to every person who needs a boost in their faith system, who yearns to move to the next level and or dimension in their life.

To my mother and late grandmothers whose faith in God made a great impact on my life. It was their belief in God as well as their trust in Him which has laid a foundation for my spiritual walk with God. They never gave up no matter how hard and despondent their life seemed in the natural. They stuck it out until change happened.

To my daughter Janelle I dedicate this book. The anointing of God is upon your life. The assignment that God has on your life must come to fulfillment. ...and the devil has just lost another battle.

Last but by no means least; I dedicate this book to the Governor and Lord of my life, Jesus Christ. Who has faith in me to deposit this book into my spirit and directs me to bring it to his people. One day I sought a "word" from God as I normally do. I had completed the manuscript but was procrastinating as to the next step. So I said, Lord I know you give me a "word" everyday but give me something different today and show me what to do with it. Randomly I open the Bible and a scripture which was previously highlighted came into focus, Psalm 68:11KJV. "The Lord gave the word: great was the company of those that published it. I said, "Yes Lord I hear you loud and clear" then close the Bible. I didn't need a clearer word than that. But I prefer the Amplied version which is; "The Lord gives the word [of power]; the women who bear and publish [the news] are a great host. So here I am obedient to voice of God.

Acknowledgments

Heartfelt thanks to everyone who spiritually supported me or contributed in anyway to the development of this project.

Janelle Boxhill (my daughter) – graphics

Pastor Barrington Goldson, Calvary Tabernacle, Hempstead, NY) – for reading the first draft and for your suggestion.

Pastor Donald Vereen, Lighthouse Christian Ministries, Bakersfield, CA. – for reading the final draft of this project.

Prudence Campbell – Props

Deon and Emily Thomas – in whose house I lived on Martha's Vineyard where this book came to "life."

Clarence & Lawrence Watson (brothers) – financial contribution and literary resource respectively.

Eleanor Pearlson, Kim and Leighton Todd, Rosalyn and Denamos Moore, Jill and Johnathan Bernstein, Claudette Davis and to everyone whose is not mentioned here, your input was greatly appreciated.

CONTENTS

FAVOR

June 2005 God took me from New York City, where I lived since 1992 and 'threw' me on the island of Martha's Vineyard, in Massachusetts. I intended to spend two months which ended into two years. God provided favor to me in many ways through various people whom has come across my path. There was an incident which took place, which in a sense was beyond my control. There was a resolution made and the terms agreed upon. It was the final day of the terms of agreement; I had taken care of my responsibility, but the enemy in his means to discredit me caused the other party to err in their responsibility and therefore my input was gone unnoticed. Therefore they thought I had forfeit my agreement and decided to take further steps. God sent someone from the 'enemy's' camp to let me know what the enemy was planning. I was then able to clarify the situation and prevent further outburst. (I have never met nor do I know this person). Now what do you call it when the adversary's agent tries to protect you? I call that FAVOR from God.

Authority

Acts 1:8 states that when you receive the gift of the Holy Ghost you shall receive power. Power is somewhat synonymous with authority, but there is a slight difference. Power is having the ability and capability to do something. You have influence over people's actions and situations. Authority gives you permission or the right to execute the power or control that you have.

Wednesday August 21, 2002 I was baptized for the second time in my life (an adult). The first time was when I was about 12 years old. I can clearly remember how weightless and peaceful I felt. Five days after making that decision to follow God's principles, something strange happened to me. Monday Aug. 26th after leaving work, my daughter, my aunt and I went to a business meeting around 8:00 pm. The meeting ended around 10:00pm so I took my aunt to her home and then my daughter I went home. Shortly after I got home and was settling down (this was about 11:00pm) I started to feel weird, cold and disconcerted. The palms of my hands were literally white as a clean white sheet. There was no visible trace of pink or red that signifies blood. By this time I could hardly speak or even sit up in bed. I tried whatever home remedies I could find, but I was trying to treat something which I haven't a clue what it was. My body was so cold that in the month of August in New York City I was in winter socks, pajama, robe, I was under sheet, comforter and blanket and was still freezing. My daughter didn't know what to do but did the best she could and I could sense she was scared. All I could do now was lay on the bed with my bible on my chest (unable to read it). The only words I could say, just a little above whisper and with much effort (those who really know me knows that I have a high pitch voice) were "JESUS help me" as many times that I could.

I must have fallen off to sleep because the next thing I remembered was that I was kicking and throwing the layers of covers off me as I was feeling hot. That was about 1:00am Tuesday. The next day I went to work and there was a co-worker to whom I told my experience. The night I was baptized I was wearing a ring which was supposedly for protection from demons, (phooh). I had taken off all the jewelry that I had on. When I got home I got the inspiration that I don't need the ring has I have the Holy Spirit within me. So I put it down, did not discard it. So here comes the devil in the form of my co-worker telling me to wear the ring because you got it for a purpose. Now she was professing to be a "Christian" but all she was is a regular church goer. Anyway I went home and put it back on for a couple days. But I was being convicted so much, because the Spirit of God keeps telling me to take it off. I am your only protection. So I took it off. Still didn't throw it away. The following week Monday night I was home and my daughter was grooming my hair, when I started to feel a strange feeling slowly creeping upon my body just like the incident the week before. I remember I was talking to a friend of mine on the phone and I told her what was happening to me and she was literally scared she said. Because we both believed that the devil was attacking me. I had to stop doing what I was doing and went under the hot shower. While I was under the shower I was calling out to God to deliver me. Shortly after, I felt revived. You see the devil got mad because I was not letting him have his way. During this second week of walking with God I was reaching out and seeking God more and more. I went and took the ring and down into the garbage it went. The second attack was around the same time as the first. Everything went well for the rest of the week.

On the third Monday I decided that whatever it is that is trying to get me to defy God I am going to destroy it. About an hour before the time of the previous attacks I started to walk around my apartment praying, praising and pleading the blood of Jesus Christ against Satan. And from that day there as never been another incident. You see I used the power and authority that God gave me to attack and destroy the devil's plan. At the name of Jesus demons have to flee, because his name has power and his blood gives authority by way of the Holy Ghost to use the Power. I took on Jesus' name when I received the baptism of the Holy Ghost, and that's how I have authority.

Inspiration

Long before I decided to live by God's principles and to do His Will, he gave me numerous inspirations. When I came back to the path of loving and living by His precepts he continued to give me more inspirations which I wrote down on just about any piece of paper I could find. In the winter of 2005, God gave me the insight to do this project, this book. Without His input, I wouldn't be able to put this many words on paper. I never thought I could write a book. All the ideas he gave me in the pass, he brought back to my attention (because I had written them down) and directed me to use them in this project. I never had to think hard to get thoughts to write about. Every step of the way he provided more and more motivation.

Treasure

This book has been in the spirit while I was in New York but came to life during my stay on Martha's Vineyard, Massachusetts. I guess with a lot of time to spare in the fall/winter season I was able to have communion with God much more than normal. Which was very good, because I could not find a church where I could be fed the Word like I was used to. I had to live off the reserve that I had until I could get to someplace where people really want to worship God. I had learned to seek God for myself, so therefore I can worship him by and for myself. I can clearly remember one Sunday I was about to leave for church (on the Vineyard) and an unusual feeling of peace, joy and happiness all in one came over me. In trying to contain myself as well as to comprehend the feeling that came over me, I paused for a moment, because I could not remember feeling that way before. I asked God "what is the meaning of this?" His response was, "I will let you reap in places you did not sow." That's exactly what was happening. Everything that I had access to and was open up to me was nothing that I had previously contributed to, but I was reaping. I had to take a praise break. I probably scared the neighbors but God had to get His glory.

Solomon wrote in proverbs 13:22b (AMP) that the wealth of the sinner [finds its way eventually] into the hands of the righteous, for whom it was laid up; those that love God and are chosen by him. God spoke through his prophet Isaiah (chapter 45:2-3) saying "I will go before thee and make the crooked places straight: I will break in pieces the gates of brass and cut in sunder the bars of iron. And I will give thee the treasures of darkness and hidden riches of secret places that thou mayest know that I, the Lord which call thee by thy name, am the God of Israel."

Hope

October 23, 2004 I was participating in a prayer service which was a part of ten days of fasting and prayer at the church I was a member of (Calvary Tabernacle) in Hempstead, New York. At a certain point in the service Pastor instructed us to kneel down and wait for a word from God. He further said that we shouldn't say anything but to wait for the word. While I was waiting I was inspired with thoughts of what a friend is, based on different scriptures and then it stopped. With my presumptuousness I spoke inwardly, "God is that it?" At that time I heard pastor said, "don't get up until you get the word. I knew that was not 'the' word so I waited. Shortly after that I heard the words "earthen vessel." Right away my focus went to the scripture where God instructed Jeremiah to get an earthen bottle.... (Jeremiah19). So I said this could not be my word

Lord because from memory that scripture was dealing with damnation/doom. I was impatient but God continued because he showed me a clay jar which was whole and then it was smashed in pieces. Immediately I saw two hands with palms up and the pieces of clay started to form back into a jar. What was significant about this picture was that as the jar was being re-shaped that there was transformation taking place simultaneously. A different color and quality jar but similar shape. It was now a jar that resembles that of choice china. It bears the colors of royal blue and white. After the transformation had been completed, the masterpiece was hoisted and I could see two shelves toward the ceiling and the jar was placed between the shelves. At this point I was in awe at what had taken place. Then I heard these words; "when the world pass and see you, they will know that it is I God who did this." Translation: after he has broken me he takes the broken pieces of my life and reshapes them. While he his sculpting he converts me into something of greatest value- his masterpiece for his glory. So though I might have similar traits of the former object yet the quality, characteristics and the appearance has been upgraded only because of the Master's hands.

Hope is saying NO when your past is trying to control your future. Therefore I have high hopes that God has an expected end for my life.

INTRODUCTION

Faith "sees"[1] the invisible, believes the incredible and receives the impossible. God can take a dead/barren situation and bring life from it. This is referred to in Isaiah 54 and Ezekiel 36:36-38. It is up to us to walk by Faith and not by sight (2 Cor.5:7). Therefore I don't object to waiting upon God until he sees it fit for him to make the impossible possible. Everything I need to survive in this lifetime is already provided in the spiritual realm. If it is provided in the spiritual, then it is just a matter of time before it is manifested in the natural. The beautiful flower you see today, was once [hidden in] a bud. The flower could not be seen readily, because it was enveloped in a protective sheath to keep it intact until the time of flowering. The natural eye was unable to see the "flower", but it was the intent of the spiritual realm that a flower will come to perfection at the right time.[2] The spiritual realm has always been aware of its existence. If you could see the miracle of a single flower clearly, your whole life would change.[3]

It's easy to "advise" others on what to do or not to do. However when it becomes personal, it is not so easy to take your own advice. In your lowest of low, God has someone set apart to speak on your behalf.[4] Sometimes you think life as dealt with you harshly and you just want to quit. You want to trade your Faith in God for past happiness, so you resort to returning to the place where you once left. I make reference to Naomi who lost her husband, both sons, as well as her hope in God. She decided to go back to the place where God had brought her from and so she wanted her two daughters-in-laws to leave her and "get a life". What she didn't know, was that it was God's intention to bring her to the land of Moab so that she could form an unbreakable bond with Ruth. Faith is getting under somebody whose wings has "fallen down" and push their vision. Though that person's vision may be laid aside, God is able to bring back that vision to life. Just like how God used Ruth to do for Naomi. The devil wanted to abort what God intended for Naomi, by trying to get Ruth to turn back.[5] When you are going through the storms and the tornadoes of your life, remember that God allows them to happen for a change to come in your life. This change causes the "dead" branches and junk in your life to be separated from you, so you can spring up and flourish and bear good fruit. In the book of John 15:1-2, Jesus is quoted as saying that, "He is the true vine and is Father is the husbandman. Any branch that bears not fruit will be removed and the branch that bears fruit he purges so it may bring forth more fruit". Don't cry bitter tears just yet, wait for the vision, it will come.

Faith is trusting that God gives you his vision for you to birth here on earth. It is His vision so he has already provided the necessary provisions to foster the vision. When God shows you the vision he gives you a picturesque summary of what is to be. What he does not show you are the obstacles that you will encounter. But as long as you have faith in Him, you will overcome the obstacles along your journey. Recently I watched a supposedly comedy/movie. I bought it because I wanted to watch something hilarious. This movie was far from what I expected anyway. [6]There was a rich tycoon who owned a casino/hotel in Las Vegas, Nevada. He was uncomfortably wealthy and just didn't know what to do with his money. So he planned a contest where six people who entered his casino were randomly selected. These six people where given a key to a locker in Silver City, New Mexico. The first person to open the box would find $2 million in cash which was the prize money. This man was having fun watching the progress of the competition with his friends; who gambled as to who will be the winner. This was a high stakes race where winnings were concerned. He was giving away money to his friends for just about any little silly game they came up with.

Each contestant faced and conquered different obstacles enroute to the prize. These obstacles were not a part of the competition. They were just a part of life obstacles which just happened.

Now in Silver City, New Mexico there was a fundraiser in aid of Feeding the less-fortunate Children, in progress. It so happen that all twelve (number increased from six) arrived at the designated place where the prize money was stashed, at the same time. They decided and agreed to share the money amongst themselves. God allowed a turn of event and they all landed on stage of the fundraiser with $2 million dollars in their possession. There was a mis-communication between the contestants and the fundraisers and the money was eventually donated to the children without them (contestants) realizing what was taking place. They finally decided to give up their winnings to a worthy cause.

This vision was financially supported because the casino tycoon promised involuntarily to match every dollar that was donated to the fundraiser. They received over $5 million. The lesson here is, God is faithful and the vision to feed the children is his vision, but he entrusted it to this person whom he chose to be a "power of attorney" for Him on earth. Therefore he provided the provision long before the vision was entrusted to His elect. Look closely at the word PROVISION. PRO = prerequisite = before. A condition has to be met before some thing happens. Vision = idea or revelation. So PROVISION means before the vision I God provides.

You see good things take a while to occur but great things appear suddenly. That's how God works. So all you have to do is let your faith work for you. Christians (I mean people who have accepted the Salvation plan and is actively serving God) may sometimes become complacent and tend to slack up in their faith. So their faith becomes either "little" or they have "none". Jesus refers to this attitude of faith many times in the Bible. However the non-Christians who receive blessings / miracles from God has receive such because of their (and I quote from Jesus) "great" faith.

CHAPTER 1
FAITH

When God created mankind he used his hands to mold the anatomy. He blew his breath into the nostrils and man received life. This depicts God's hands-on, intimate relationship with his masterpiece. Not only did he framed man with is own hands but he also add His (God's) image and likeness to the prototype. Given all the effort and details that was put into creating and making man, it goes to show that God's intention was that man share an intimate relationship with him. Because of the 'fall' of man, the relationship was estranged. But he made provision that mankind can rise from the 'fall' and be reunited with him as was his original plan.

When you decide to turn from left to "right" and walk with God, you accept him as Lord and Savior. He then blows his breath into you for the second time, but this time in the form of the Holy Ghost. My, my, my, God is an intimate God; he does everything on the inside of you. His love for you goes way back before you were ever born. Like he told Jeremiah which applies to you, is that he knew that you would be in existence long before there was a meeting of the 'bodies'.[7] Not only does he know your origin but he also knows your end. He chose the sperm that contributed to your existence out the millions of sperm that were competing for the prize. What you do with His choice for your life is entirely up to you. Again he speaks promise and life to Jeremiah, that the ending of his life is already designed.[8] All you have to do is to trust him as well as trust in him. No matter what kind of challenges come your way, believe that God has already made a way of escape. All the potholes and obstacles that you encounter on the road of life will transform into stepping stones towards your victory. Amen.

As with the heroes and heroines of the Bible, Faith can open up different channels from which result various ministries. You will be elevated to a higher level in Jesus Christ. It might some how seems insignificant to you at that moment, when you are being empowered to take action but afterwards it will all make sense. Remember God's thoughts and actions are not graspable by mankind. He is in a league of his own which is called Infinity. Man sees and thinks within a limited scope. He/She cannot operate outside the box call perception. God knows and sees more than we can ever imagine. He knows what will happen in the future because in fact, he is the future. With limited ability you say, if I don't see it or cannot touch it, it does not exist. If I cannot perceive it, it will never happen. Paul gave a reminder in 2 Corinthians 4:18 that you should not focus on the things which can be seen by the physical eyes, because they only last for a while. You should place emphasis on the spiritual things which can not be seen with the physical eyes but with the spiritual eye, as these are eternal. 1Corinthians 2:9 states that, eye hath not seen, nor ear heard, neither have entered into the heart of man, the things which God hath prepared for them that love him.

CHAPTER 2
WHAT IS FAITH?

Faith is a choice which comes from the heart. It is an integral part of serving God. Without Faith there is no way you can please him, absolutely not. It is impossible.[9] It is the essence, the basis or the core of things that you hope for with the proof, the verification or the confirmation of things not seen. That is, Faith is the foundation on which your anticipation is established. You cannot see the future or the result with your physical eyes and there is nothing you can actually 'hold on to' but there is an instinct which goes beyond your natural vision. Faith is not dependent on man's physical ability to see or his ability to acquire knowledge of things. However it is connected to his belief system and his capability to activate his belief. Martin Luther King Jr. said "Take the first step in Faith. You don't have to see the staircase, just take the first step". Don't let fear of the unknown; rob you of your blessings. Go get it!

Faith is one of the nine aspects of the Fruit of the Spirit. {The Fruit of the Spirit is a prerequisite for the Gifts of the Spirit}. I call this type of Faith, learned faith. It takes much discipline to learn this Faith. Gradually, with personal experiences and that of others it becomes learned. There are nine Gifts of the Spirit and its no coincidence that Faith is one of them. This Faith I call, graduated faith. For someone to be bestowed with the gift of Faith, that person have to possess the Fruit of the Spirit (all nine aspects together). When you achieve that level of the gift of Faith, it is that you can withstand any storm, stare in the face of any adversity or whatever challenge you are faced with, without second guessing if God can. But you stand firm, calm and collective with the assurance that, **my God will!** James spoke about this type of faith that the temptations and trials that we encounters, it teaches us patience (long suffering) (James 1:2 & 3).

CHAPTER 3
ILLUSTRATION OF THE FRUIT
OF THE SPIRIT

To illustrate the fruit of the Spirit,[10] I use a hand of ripe banana with nine fingers. Each banana represents an attribute of the Spirit. The thick band of "flesh" that holds the fingers in place, I call Perseverance.[11] As with the natural banana, the ripening stage does not occur simultaneously. If you look closely when the banana is in this stage you will see that some fingers have more green color than some. They all have reached the ripening stage, but some mature faster than some. When the bananas are all completely ripen, they hold together and will not become loose, unless disturbed by some type of pressure no matter how slight. When one finger becomes dislocated, the chemistry has been disrupted. The bond becomes weak therefore you have one banana falling from the cluster and then another and another and another.

The nine attributes of the Spirit does not come to perfection all at once. Some require more time and work to reach the ripening or matured stage. Once they reach maturation they all have to work together to be effective. With Perseverance hard at work, the fruit of the Spirit all work together for good to those who love God and abide by his principles.

The question one might ask or thought about is. How do I acquire Faith, can it be bought? Here goes, the only way to get Faith is through the Salvation Plan. Which is Repent, be Baptized and be filled with the gift of the Holy Ghost. This is the foundation of Faith. In Acts 1:4-8 after Jesus' resurrection, he spoke with his disciples and they inquired as to the restoration of the kingdom of Israel. And he answered, "It is not for you to know the times or the seasons, which the Father hath put in his own power. But ye shall receive power, after the Holy Ghost is come upon you: and ye shall be witnesses unto me in Jerusalem, Judea, Samaria and unto the uttermost part of the earth. Hebrews chapter 11:1 tells us that Faith is the substance of things hope for, the evidence of things not seen. These men had hopes that the kingdom of Israel would be restored and were trying to get the evidence which is Jesus' word as to when he would rebuild.

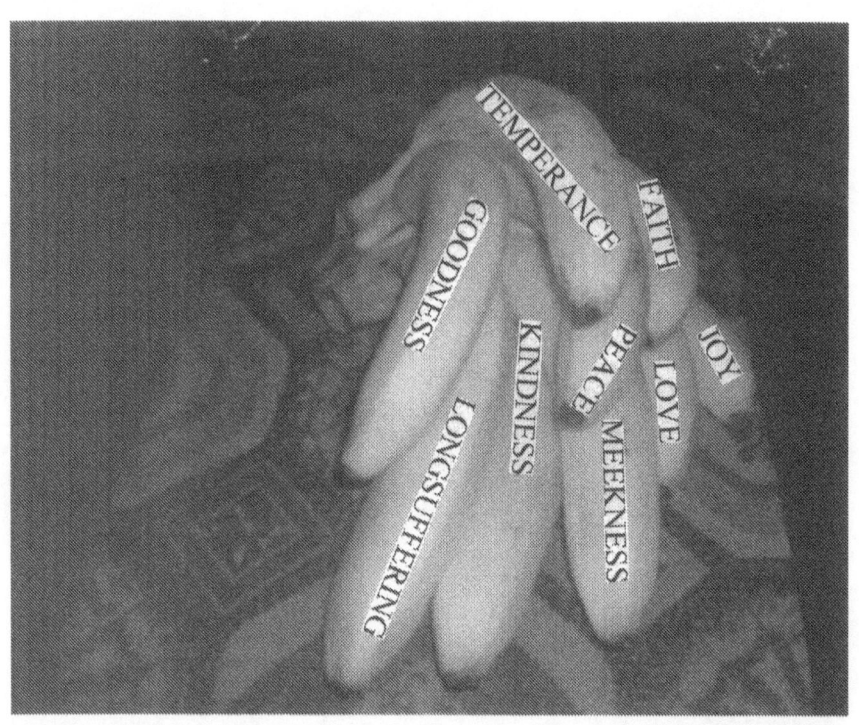

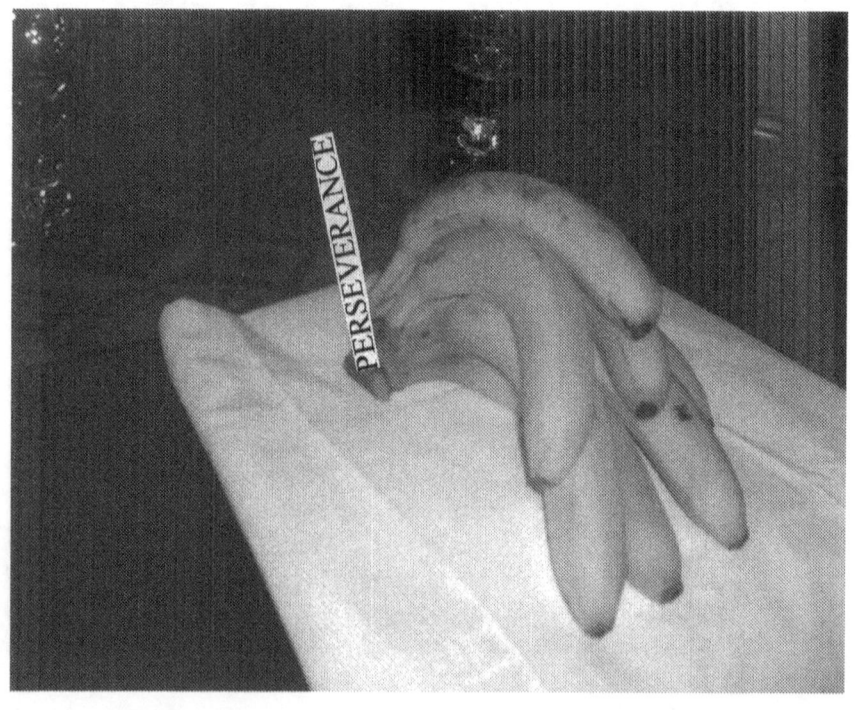

The disciples were already repented and baptized with water but had not yet received the gift of the Holy Ghost. Why had they not received the Holy Ghost? Because Jesus had not yet return to his Heavenly Father after his resurrection. Therefore the Holy Ghost could not be released onto man. In verse 6 Jesus spoke of the baptism of the Holy Ghost, because he knew that he was leaving earth soon and while he was here the Holy Ghost could not appear. The disciples had hoped and believed Jesus' prophesies but without the Holy Ghost the most important part could not happen. That is, the Action could not become a reality.

For us to develop faith we must first know the Word. Without the Word, Faith does not exist. John wrote that the Word was at the start of creation and the Word was with God. Then the Word manifested into human form and dwelt among us being full of grace and truth.[12] Jesus is the word made flesh who creates and brings our faith to perfection and maturity.[13]

God has more faith in us than we have in ourselves. He allows the trials, temptations, storms, whatever you may call them, because he has confidence that we will fight the good fight of faith and not fall victim to the devil. The devil only picks on those whom he knows have faith in God. Remember Job, it was Satan who challenged God that Job was not faithful has he seemed to be. God allow Satan to touch Job but there was a limit. You see there is a limit to what the devil can do but there is no limit to what God can do. Satan can not touch you if God does not allow it. God will not allow more than you can withstand. There is no affliction, complication or trials that can attack you that is not common to mankind. There is nothing new in life even though man has encountered certain complications and is confused. Somewhere along the way, someone had to undergo similar complications.

Satan has never learned from Job's encounter and still does not understand that when he interferes with God's people that what he his doing is helping them to go to the next level in God. At the end of Job's ordeal he was blessed by God, twice as much as that which was taken from him.

CHAPTER 4
FAITH IS A GIVEN

Faith applies to Christians as well as non-Christians. It is not just a 'churchy' thing. The US Federal Government publicly puts its faith in God. Hence the US currency bears the logo(s) /words IN GOD WE TRUST. The national Pledge of the USA also highlights that the pacesetters of this country truly had faith in a higher power (which is God) to whom man is subservient to in all matters of his life. Therefore the words "one nation under God" emphasizes their belief even to this day. So no matter what the controversy is today whether to separate or not, it still remains, **One Nation under God.**

Faith is an ability or reflex that each person possesses whether it is positively or negatively used. It is trusting in someone or something that will produce positive results. Positive results vary from person to person. Why is that so? Because your rival may do something against you expecting to get positive results from his/her actions. That action taken by your rival is negative in your perspective, but in that person's thoughts it is positive if the intended result is achieved. The successful person, who does not believe in God, does however believe in what he does and expects that it will produce positive results. He/ She cannot see the end result of his expectations but believe that it will happen. Let me throw this in as extra.

Fear

Contrary to what people think, Fear is not the opposite of Faith. Fear is doubting oneself. Fear has caused man to become their greatest enemy against themselves. The acronym which has been coined for FEAR is false evidence appearing real. Fear is expressing 'faith' in anticipation of some unknown pain, danger or event, accompanied by the desire to flee or fight. This is how I view Fear. It is failed expectations as (the) result of your lack of faith. Your emotions lead you to believe that something is going to happen. Picture this; Fear is like an angry, hungry lion on the attack, with a cold stare on its face. Jaws open wide exposing sharpened fangs, ready for action like a lethal weapon. All it is is a delusion.

When you accept fear, you made it your leader because it controls you. You gave it power and authority to destroy your life. But when the love of God shows up in your situation you realize that all it (fear) was was a figment of your imagination. No longer is fear in the forefront, but it dissipates and disappears out of mind.

Someone once wrote: Fear knocks at the door
Faith answered,
And found no one there.

Anonymous

Fear is of the devil. Faith is of God. So I'll rephrase this quote:
Fear (devil) knocks at the door
Faith (God) answers,
And found no one there.

Fear and doubt work together and so does faith and hope. So when you let God answers the devil's knocks then all you will have is Hope. Fear is a stronghold of the devil. You give the devil the okay to drive fear into you. He throws it out but who receive it? My mom told me this, "the devil says he tempts you but he never forces you." It was your decision.

Side Effects Of Fear

Fear is a phantom disease. If not dispelled from your system you begin to worry and eventually will develop into different emotional disorders and or other deficiencies. Such as anger, anxiety, depression, stress, etc. These effects will gradually transform the body's health system to disorders like heart attack, ulcers, diabetes, hypertension, eating disorders, backache gastrointestinal abnormalities, to name a few. Some people may be unable to control their emotions and may lead to murder or suicide. Fear will make you mentally unstable. You can eliminate ill-health, enjoy life and live longer by simply having faith and dispel fear. Remember whatever is not of faith is sin.

Therefore when illusion shows up, counteract it with your faith in God. Why? Because God did not give you the spirit of fear. What he gave you is the spirit of power, the spirit of love and the spirit of a sound mind.[14] Fear makes you crazy. So bind the spirit of fear with the spirit of power so you will have a sound mind and will be able to love yourself as well as others. *Now that we have an awareness of fear, let's get back to the subject of Faith.*

Everyday you exercise faith without even realizing that you do. These are some instances where people practice faith without realizing they do. (1)When you go to sleep at 'nights' anticipating that "tomorrow when I wake I am going to do...." (2) Every person would like to have a piece of the American dream. So you decide to get a mortgage on a house hoping that at the end of 15 or 30 years you will pay off the Bank and be the rightful owner of the house. (3) A pregnant mother believes that the child she is carrying in her womb will be sweet, loving, and good and even sometimes have the fetus attending college before birth. (4)When you go to sit you believe that you will be supported by the chair and will not end up on the floor doing a somersault. (5)You make business decisions and plans for the next five years and you expect that during this time period you might not make a profit. But you anticipate that in the fifth year that "your ship will come in". You expect that your business will yield the profits that your plans had illustrated. (6) When heads of government meet on Official business, it is the host country's responsibility to ensure the safety of its guest(s). Now if the guest(s) did not have faith in their host, that their safety is secured, they would not agree to go. The reality and fact is that in the next three minutes after your decision making, your heart might just stop working and that would be the end of your life's dreams. But you have enough faith not to focus on death because if you do, you would give up trying. God gives to every man a measure of faith (Romans 12:3). Your focus should be on what you want to achieve and your determination will allow you to be persistent and consistent in whatever you do.

Abraham Lincoln the 16th President of the United States of America was considered a sceptic who suffered depression throughout his life.[15] He however accepted God's Devine will in his life. Abraham shows how suffering can be bound up with spiritual purpose. From his suffering experience he realized happiness along with humility and determination. He believed that he was not the governor of his life, and despite whatever means he came about to being, that there is a Devine force that is responsible for his existence. He believed that he had a job to do in his lifetime and not to be an idle onlooker.

In the Summer of 1863, with the activity of the Civil War, President Lincoln was faced with fires all around him. In early July, high-priced military victories at Vicksburg, Mississippi and at Gettysburg, Pennsylvania, opened an opportunity; Lincoln thought to end the war. When the opportunity was lost, he described himself "oppressed" and in "deep distress". Around the same time, draft riots in New York City, brought this city to its knees in bitter anti-black violence, and emphasized the ongoing horror. With the profound pressure facing him, he became greatly saddened and found peace by acknowledging his own powerlessness. According to General James F. Rusling, President Lincoln said that during the fighting at Gettysburg he turned to prayer. Lincoln felt the whole thing to be in God's hands and somehow a sweet comfort crept into his soul."

In another revealing incident that summer, Elizabeth Keckly, Mary Lincoln's dressmaker, watched the president drag himself into the room where she was fitting the First Lady. "His step was slow and heavy, and his face sad", Keckly recalled. "Like a tired child he threw himself upon a sofa and shaded his eyes with his hands. He was a complete picture of dejection. Lincoln announced that he had just returned from the War Department, where the news was "dark, dark everywhere." Then he took a small Bible from a stand near the sofa and began to read. "A quarter of an hour passed and on glancing at the sofa the face of the President seemed more cheerful", Keckly remembered. The dejected look was gone and his countenance was lighted up with new resolution and hope." Wanting to see what he was reading, Keckly pretended she had dropped something and went behind where Lincoln was sitting so she could look over his shoulder. It was the Book of Job.

Here are some examples of people in the Bible who had Faith in God whether they were his disciples or not. Abraham, whom God called his friend, was obedient and willing to sacrifice his heir. The rich Centurion who was not a follower of God but had faith that Jesus could heal his servant. The Syro-Phoenician (Gentile) woman whose daughter was demon possessed went in search of Jesus to heal her daughter. If an unbeliever can have faith so can the believer who trust in God. Can God trust you to trust your Faith in him? Can he brag about you and volunteer you like he did with Job to the adversary?

In a speech made to the boys of Winston Churchill's old school, Harrow, on October 29, 1941 he advised them to "Never give in, never, never, never, never. In nothing great or small, large or petty. Never give in except to convictions of honor and good sense. Never yield to force; never yield to the apparently overwhelming might of the enemy." This speech is one of perseverance and faith and though it might seem simple it carries great advice. Don't give up when the going gets tough, dark and dreary. With prayer as your comfort and the Bible as your guide and your weapon, persevere and you will find an alternate route to your destination. Let nothing or no one keep you from your destiny. It is you're your God given right. The devil will put obstacles in your way to prevent you from reaching your goal. Obstacles can be in the form of a job lack, limitation, kin folks or even followers of Christ ("church people") to name a few. Do not let the obstacle label you as unclean or unworthy. If you have to crawl on all fours to get your portion, do so. You have to outsmart the opposition. Name your victory, sneak up when they are otherwise engaged and claim your victory in Jesus' name. Never let fear prevent you from moving ahead, because your opportunity only passes your route once, so grasp it.

CHAPTER 5
DON'T CAST BLAME....

Never let unfair circumstances lead you to blame your oppressors and become discouraged and give up on yourself. God will use you to do great things despite your earlier rejection. God had to use someone or something to move you from your comfort zone, so he can process and prepare you for the future. There was a fairytale I read when I was knee high many, many years ago. A little chicken named Henny Penny felt something hit her on the head. She did not know what it was. Immediately she jumped into action. She was going to let the king know that the sky was falling and that something needed to be done. Sometimes God will get your attention and move you away from your present location for different reasons. Maybe to prevent greater danger or take you to the place where you need to be, or that your present location is your destiny but that you need to be separated from your environ so has to be empowered for the "job" or just to teach you common sense. The story of Jephthah (Judges 11) depicts how Jephthah was angry with his brethren for throwing him out of his father's land. Because he was focusing on the hurt and anger he felt, he could not see that it was set up by God. That he will be highly revered by not only his brothers but the country as well, in the future.

Joseph, the son that Jacob loved most of all his twelve children, was sold into Egypt for twenty pieces of silver, by ten of his brothers. As the story goes, Joseph went through many changes in his lifetime. He eventually became ruler over Egypt and later saved the life of is family including the ten that plotted against him.[16] He realized that he was displaced from his father's land to be placed in his destined position for the greater good.[17]

God will bring you at times to a place of powerlessness, so you can exercise Faith in him. Put not your trust in man whose breath is in his nostrils, who has no power of his own but rely upon God to empower him. When you pray in faith, God will change your life immediately.[18] Isaiah prophesied that before you call unto God with your petition he will answer; and while you are still talking to Him he will respond.[19] He is spontaneous in his doings. Do not put your trust in things or man but in God and God alone.

CHAPTER 6
THE MIND - A TERRIBLE "THING" TO WASTE.

The mind is an invisible organ which plays a very important role in our lives every single day and night. Whether we are of Christian faith, Judaism, Muslims, Hinduism, Buddhist, Mormons, Jehovah's Witness, Agnostic and Atheist to name a few, we all accept that we have a mind which controls us. Literally, one would say we are crazy to think that something that does not exist physically can control humans. It is said that the mind is where all battles are won or lost. The adversary cannot know your thoughts if you don't share it with him / her. [But I have never shared with the devil.] Yes you do. Each time that you open your mouth and express your fear and doubt about a situation, you have invited the devil to be apart of your decision making. Death and life is in the power of your tongue, so saith Solomon the wisest man who ever lived.[20] (Proverbs 18:21). James also allude to the effect of the tongue, that it is full with deadly poison.[21]

The devil at times will let you feel that you have no faith because you don't have a house, car, job, a spouse, flashy wardrobe, child(ren) etc. This is carnal thinking and that means self is in control and not God. Apostle Paul tells us about carnal thinking in Romans 8 verse 7. By- pass the carnal thinking, cut deep into the spirit mind and listen for that still soft voice when God is talking to you. So God can work in and through you the way he wants, therefore he can bless you. In 2 Chronicles 15 verses 2, Azariah prophesied to Asa, Judah and Benjamin saying, "The Lord is with you, while you be with him; and if ye seek him, he will be found of you; but if ye forsake him, he will forsake you."

Your faith should not be hung up on stuff but upon the Creator and maker of stuff that you desire. Get your mind to filter out the lies that Satan sows in it. Think of what Jesus wants you to think. You must strive to have the Mind of Christ. Keep your mind focused on God constantly. Read the Word of God frequently. Pray earnestly, not just saying words or repeating the words of others; but reverence God by pouring out your heart to him. Confess your sins and wait for his direction. Do not nag God with the same petition over and over. Because that is a sign that your faith tank as ran low. Remember, he who planted the ears can he not hear.[22]

Below is an Alleged Diagram of the Mind. (Size of circle denotes the amount of activity)

ILLUSTRATION of the MIND

Mind of Unsaved Person

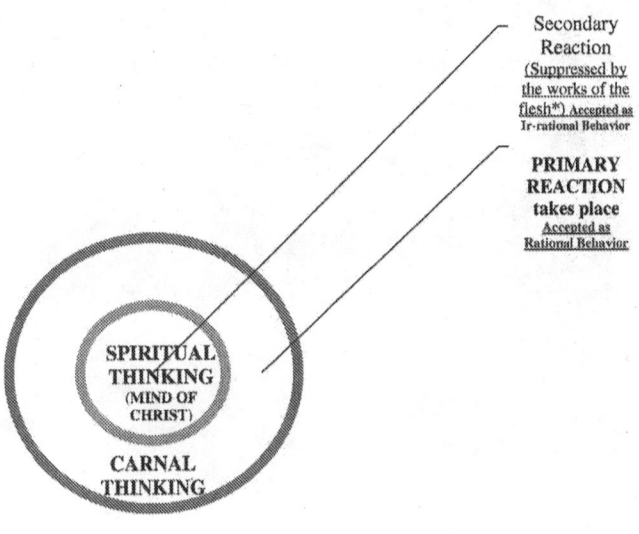

Secondary
Reaction
(Suppressed by
the works of the
flesh*) Accepted as
Ir-rational Behavior

**PRIMARY
REACTION
takes place**
Accepted as
Rational Behavior

SPIRITUAL
THINKING
(MIND OF
CHRIST)

CARNAL
THINKING

* See Figure 3

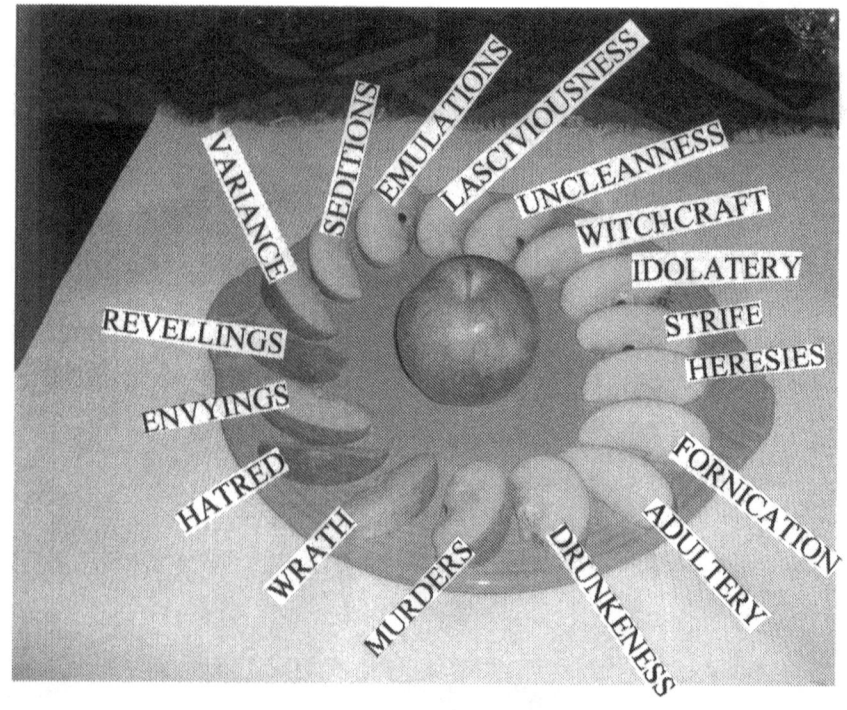

ILLUSTRATION of the MIND

Mind of the Saved Person

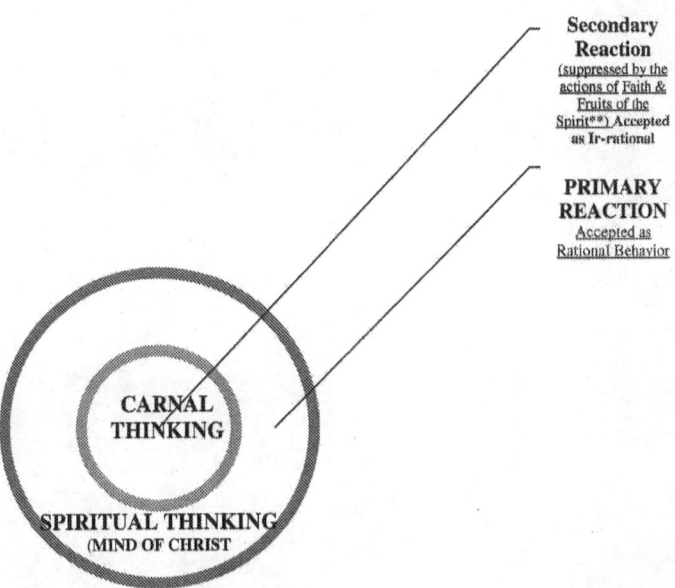

**Secondary
Reaction**
(suppressed by the
actions of Faith &
Fruits of the
Spirit**) Accepted
as Ir-rational

**PRIMARY
REACTION**
Accepted as
Rational Behavior

**CARNAL
THINKING**

SPIRITUAL THINKING
(MIND OF CHRIST

**See Figure 4

JOY
FAITH
LOVE
PEACE
MEEKNESS
TEMPERANCE
KINDNESS
GOODNESS
LONGSUFFERING

CHAPTER 7
TYPES OF FAITH

Based on the many miracles documented in the Bible which happened has a result of Faith, I have drafted some different examples of Faith. These are Anchored, Covenant, Prompted, Aroused, Great, Persevering, Little, Genuine and God-type Faith.

Covenant Faith is the Faith that Abraham displayed, when God told him to leave his familiar surrounding and people and go to a place where he would be shown. Scriptural references show how Abraham was blessed because of his faith in God. So when God told him to offer up his love-child Isaac as a burnt sacrifice he obeyed. God had promised Abraham many years back that his name would be great and in him will all the families of the earth be blessed. So he trusted God. Isaac was his heir and without his heir the covenant God made with him could not come to pass (Genesis 12). Like Abraham, Isaac's covenant faith (Genesis 26:1-25) with God initially started residual income (verses 12 & 13; ...then Isaac sowed ... and received in the same year a hundredfold) which is very much active today in our economic arena. God never utters an idle word. Every word must yield fruit. Not one of is word will return unto him void.[23] His covenant that he made with his chosen, remains in effect. Stop focus on your circumstance(s) and look at the covenant made between you and God to reinforce your faith.

Genuine Faith - Mary never doubted the angel that appeared to her and delivered the Great news.[24] She was chosen to be the mother of the Messiah. Her Faith was validated when she visited her cousin Elizabeth, who was also chosen to mother a special child named John.

23

Prompted Faith - Pharaoh the king of Egypt suffered from insecurity. He felt threatened by the children of Israel and how blessed they were. They continued to multiply despite the affliction he and his followers brought upon them. He became confused, angry and fearful so he ordered the mid-wives to kill all the Hebrew males at the time of their birth. His command was not granted. These women were more afraid of the power of God than the power of Pharaoh. But Pharaoh was persistent because he was afraid that a male child will grow up to replace him as king. He was afraid to lose power. So he ordered to kill every male child. But Moses' mother was prompted by her faith in God that he was a special child; so she hid him for three months.

When she could no longer keep him in hiding, she was prompted to design a way of escape for her son. Prompted by faith, Moses' mother 's plan led him into the house of Pharaoh (the enemy) where he was loved and raised by the king and his daughter.[25]

Anchored Faith - Noah's faithfulness and obedience made God chose him to save creation from being completely wiped out. He became the first person in history to perform a major task as building a ship as recorded in the Bible. Imagine this huge boat on land with no water in sight and all the jokes and mockery that was directed at Noah. He could have given up because this was a long term project, 120 years waiting for rain (NLT). His faith was anchored in the God he served, so he never gave up but continued his task to the desired end. He and his family were the only humans left alive after the great flood.[26]

Aroused Faith - The young son squandered his inheritance which he demanded of his father and was reduce to living in squalor eating the swines' food. He realized that he could have been home living a better live than the one shared with the swines. He decided that he would go home and repent. He believed that his father would forgive and receive him. But he knew he was not worthy of the forgiveness so he would humble himself and become a servant.

Great Faith - A Centurion whose servant was sick with palsy, sought Jesus because he believed that Jesus could make his servant well. But what was so interesting was that after entreating Jesus' help he did not want Jesus to come to his house. Why? Because he knew that his lifestyle was unworthy and he did not deserve to have such a Worthy person in his environ. But he was confident that if Jesus just commands healing in absentia that the servant would be healed at home. This amazed Jesus to know that an unrighteous person has great faith for the welfare of others.[27]

There was a woman who suffered hemorrhaging for 12 years. She probably spent all her money on trying to find relief as well as cure for her condition. For a woman and I speak for myself, the monthly menstruation can become intolerable at times especially when there is a change in cycle. Now women, this one is for you, visualize 12 years continuous bleeding without any expectation that it will stop. This woman was at her wits end. Jesus was her last straw and she decided that she was going to clutch that straw. She said, oh if I could just touch the hem, not the whole garment, not his body, but just the hem of his garment, I know that I will receive my healing. And she did touch the hem and she received what she expected. What Jesus said to her, not only was she healed but that her faith made her whole (Mark 5:25-34).

Persevering Faith - A Syrophoenician woman (considered Gentile) had a daughter who was demon- possessed. She sought Jesus' help to rid her child of the demon. Because she was not a Jew the disciples tried to turn her away. She was persistent and insisted despite being embarrassed even by the person from whom she was seeking help. She would not leave without what she came in search of, which was change in her daughter's life. She did not care if she was trespassing. She knew that this man has what her daughter needs and she was not leaving without it.[28]

Little Faith - A rich, young, religious man was unsure if his way of living would merit him eternal life. He asked of Jesus, "Good master what shall I do to inherit eternal life?" Jesus answered "Why do thou call me good"? "No one is good except God; however you must obey the commandments." The young man responded that ever since his youthful days he has lived his life in accordance to the commandments. Jesus then told him to sell all his possession and share the money amongst the poor and he will have treasure in heaven. Then come and follow me. When the man heard this he was very, very sad, because he was very, very rich. This man had just enough faith to believe that eternal life is available for him in God. He asked Jesus the question hoping that the answer would assure him that he was abiding by the principles set out by God. But his Faith was so little that he could not see beyond himself and his immediate possessions. Therefore it was hard for him to give it all away to claim the unseen eternal treasures that Jesus referred to. Other examples can be found in Matthew 14:25-32 and Matthew 17:14- 20. When our attention is focused on Jesus we accomplish what we desire of him. When we lose focus of Jesus, we start to focus on our self, then doubt creeps in and then we fail.

God-type Faith - This is having the Gift of Faith. As aforementioned, the Fruit of the Spirit is the prerequisite for the Gift of Faith. The Fruit of the Spirit comprises of nine aspects. All nine work simultaneously to be effective. Some of the people who had this faith were Stephen, Peter and Paul. They were the instruments of change that affected the lives of the people wherever they went. Believing that all things are possible through Jesus Christ and declare it with no hesitation, releases strength and power from almighty God. In Acts 1:8, Jesus spoke that power and authority comes with the Gift of the Holy Ghost. When you have the Gift of Faith you can relate to prophecies such as those the Prophets Isaiah, Jeremiah and Ezekiel spoke of.

CHAPTER 8
HISTORY OF FAITH

People of Faith are special people and so were our fore fathers. They exercised their faith in God and set a precedent for us to follow.[29] They heard, believed, and exercised faith in the Word of God. Paul said that Faith cometh by hearing the Word of God.[30] John emphasized that before the world was created, the Word was with God and the Word was God.

You know from the scriptures, that God never changes (does not break his covenant, Isaiah 55:11). He is the same God before creation and He is still the same today. He will be the same God even after the world has past. So therefore it is safe to say that faith develops when you live righteously and hears when God speaks to you and you act according to his will. This is obedience in its truest form.

Abraham in his obedience and heeding to the voice of God, offered his son Isaac, who was the 'apple of his eye' as a sacrifice. Noah's obedience and faith in God allowed him to build an Ark and saved creation from complete destruction from the great flood. Moses chose to suffer affliction with the people of God and gave up the worldly pleasures and treasures that Pharaoh offered. His faith in God spared the lives of the Children of Israel, when Moses led them through the Red Sea. These are just a few of the legends of our past, whose faith in God brought them through rough and trying times. Below is an illustration on obedience.

Illustration of Obedience vs Disobedience

Obedience ↔ separation from the world ↔ deliverance →blessing & favor (wages) Disobedience → separation → → repentance → ↑

(from God)

↓

Refuse to repent

↓

destruction (wages)

Translation: When you are obedient to the call of God on your life and separate yourself from the things the world has to offer, you will experience deliverance from the obstacles in your life. You become empowered and uplifted. So the wages you will receive for being obedient is blessings and favor. If you become disobedient for whatever reason and separate yourself from God and his Word, you will feel empty, down trodden and dry, no matter what fun you seem to think you have. But there is redemption for you. If you repent from being disobedient then you will be delivered, therefore separating yourself from the world and become one of God's selected. You start to obey God's commandments and place yourself in line for God's blessing and favor on your life. However if you refuse to repent then the wages you will receive is destruction (death). Disobedience is the core of the works of the flesh. In other words it is the central part of every work of the flesh (see Fig 5).

Obedience is fuel that keeps your faith flame alight. Disobedience is the extinguishing agent that kills the flame of your faith. Hence Solomon's proverb holds true: The light of the righteous rejoiceth: but the lamp of the wicked shall be put out (Proverbs 13:9).

Only when you are obedient can you have faith. Only when you have faith can you be obedient. Faithfulness is interrelated to obedience, which is connected to change. The key to *change* (generalized and covers various attitude/actions) in your life is obedience. Therefore when God instructs you to change it's in your best interest to do so.

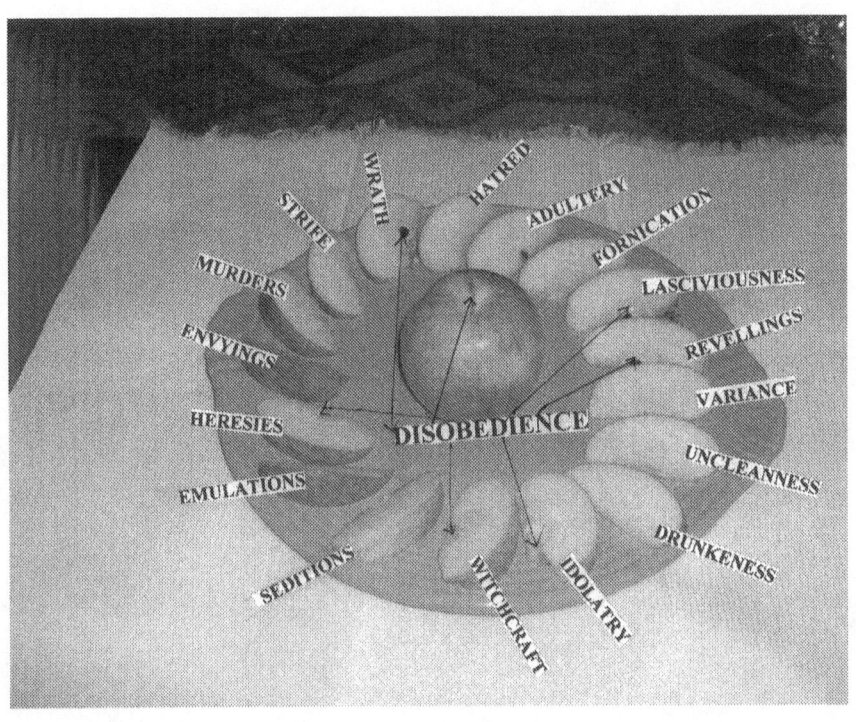

There is opportunity in the middle of every difficulty (*Anonymous*). Difficulty opens up the door for change. Recently I watched a movie in which a Fed Ex plane crashed on an island leaving one survivor cast away[31] for four years. This man had nothing (so he thought) but a few boxes which were to be delivered to customers, coconut trees with coconuts for food and liquid, dry sticks and stones from which to make fire, trees for shade and covering etc. From the boxes he had a soccer ball on which he created a face with his blood from a cut he sustained, a pair of ice skates which he used to remove the husk from the coconuts and to crack open the coconut shell so he could eat the coconut and drink the coconut water, a dress with tulle lining with which he used to catch fish. He eventually made a raft from the trees which aided in his rescue by the coast guards. The lesson here is: Everything you need to survive or to get you out of a desperate situation is around you or within your reach. All you have to do is look closer and do not be selective or prejudice or you might just miss your opportunity.

Below are some instances depicted in the Bible where the difficulty that people encountered opened doors of opportunity to them. Deuteronomy 8:18 states that, "God gives us the power to create wealth." This power is the foundation to success and prosperity.

Scriptural Reference - 2 Kings 4:7
(1) Widow

Difficulty

1. Had no money
2. Never had a job outside the home
3. Have two young sons who were going to be used as payment for debt owed.
4. She went to the prophet Elisha for help.
5. Had only one pot of oil as resource.

Opportunity: **Allow others to facilitate / participate in activities surrounding your blessing.**

The prophet told the widow to go borrow as many pots as possible from her neighbors far and wide. After that she should go inside her house with her sons and close the door then fill each borrowed pot from the one pot of oil that she has. After completing the task she went back to report to Elisha. He then told her to go and sell the pots of oil, pay her debts and to live off the rest.

Key: Obedience. This widow did not stop to think or rationalize the directive given to her by the prophet. (After all she could not come up with a solution to her situation.) She was obedient. Think about it, one pot of oil to fill many pots, does it make sense? Literally, it does not make much sense to man but because of her obedience she started her home base business, selling oil. You see, God's ways are not your ways because he does not work like man. His thoughts are not your thoughts because he does not think like man. (Isaiah 55:8).

(2)Scriptural Reference: 1 Kings 17:1-16
Widow

Difficulty

1. Had no money, no financial resource

2. Had one young son.

3. Never worked outside the home.

4. Had a handful of meal and a little oil from which to make the last meal for her son and herself and then prepare to die from hunger.

   You see no one cared for widows in those days, they were cast aside.

Opportunity: **Show kindness to (a) stranger(s) and putting aside your own need.**

She fed Elijah from the little she had for herself and her son. She showed kindness out of their need. People tend to give or help others from their abundance or from their excess blessing (see Luke 21:1-4). But extra blessings flows abundantly when you give from your needs. The result is that the widow and her son were blessed tremendously. No more lack.

Key: Obedience.

(3)Scriptural Reference- Genesis chapters 37, 39 – 45 Joseph

Difficulty:

1. Had prophetic dreams in his youth.

2. His ten older brothers hated him because their father loved him most.

3. Brothers planned to kill him but plan was aborted.

4. They then threw him in a pit.

5. They later sold him into Egypt.

6. In Egypt he was sent to prison.

7. Taken from prison to the palace and later became governor of Egypt. Joseph's prophetic dreams and the ability to translate them brought him difficulty.

Opportunity: **The ability to translate dreams afforded Joseph the opportunity to be favored by the king.** He was taken from prison and appointed to rule as governor to represent the king in Egypt. He was able to save many people's lives from starvation including his own father, brothers and their families.

Key: Obedience. Joseph was obedient to God and did not fall for Potiphar's wives adulterous plans. Because he refused her request to defile Potiphar's bed she became rejected and framed him causing him to be sent to prison. But it was because of his stay in prison and his ability to interpret dreams led Joseph to his destiny.

(4) Scriptural Reference – Job 2:10, Job 19:25-27
Job

Difficulty:

1. He was very faithful and righteous to God.

2. His children continuously sinned.

3. He continuously offer sacrifice for redemption of their sin (Job 1:5)

4. God volunteered Job to the devil.

5. He lost everything he possessed including his health and the support of his wife.

Opportunity : **To prove his obedience and faithfulness to God.**

Job's children weren't in the least bit as reverent to God as their father did. Job had to continuously counteract their sinful actions for their protection. No wonder why God had to volunteer Job to Satan. Before God allowed the devil to touch Job's possession, he (devil) could not touch anything Job had because Job was blessed by God and an hedge (wall of protection) was placed around him. So therefore all Job's possession and his children were included in the hedge. God saw the struggle and pressure that Job had to undergo with his disobedient children so he used Satan to bring difficulty into Job's life therefore relieving him of his burdens that his children caused him.

Key: Obedience. Job was later blessed twice as much of which he had before Satan attacked him, because of Job's obedience to God to pray for his friends (Job 42: 10-15).

(5)Scriptural Reference – Ruth Chapters 1 & 2
Ruth

Difficulty:

1.   Widowed

2.   Took care of her mother-in-law (Naomi) who was also a widow.

3.   Had no financial resource / no income.

4.   Never worked outside the home.

5.   She was loving and loyal to Naomi.

Opportunity: **To provide for someone other than herself.**

Ruth went to Boaz's field to secure food for her mother-in-law and herself to eat. This was told to Boaz who was impressed of such selfless attitude of Ruth. She had the opportunity to go and find another husband and to leave Naomi but refused Naomi's offer. She chose to stay and took care of Naomi. Ruth later became Mrs. Boaz and the rest is history. See Ruth chapter 4 and St. Matthew 1: 5 -17.

Key: Obedience (to Naomi) the intent at first for going to Boaz's field was not to attract him but to feed themselves. They were taken care of for the rest of their lives.

(6) Scriptural Reference – The book of Esther.
Esther

Difficulty:

1. Orphaned

2. Raised by her cousin Mordecai.

3. Her people were living in fear of being persecuted

4. She was very beautiful maiden.

5. Became a contestant to be chosen as queen.

Opportunity: To become queen to save her people from persecution.

Esther became a contestant among the beautiful maidens for the chance to be chosen as Queen. She went through 12 months of purification and grooming before appearing before the king. Favor was shown to her by the king's aide who instructed her on the appropriate attire and actions that would please the king. She was chosen as queen over 127 provinces from India to Ethiopia. She inherited much wealth and was highly revered. She was able to achieve her goal of freeing her people from the enemy.

Key: Obedience to Mordecai and to the king's aide.

If you are obedient to God, *He will guide you along the best pathway for your life.* He will advise you and watch over you." Psalm 32: 8, NLT, *For nothing is impossible with Him.* Luke 1: 37, NLT, *For he is your rock, your fortress, your deliverer, your God, your strength, in whom you will trust... the horn of your salvation, and your high tower.* Psalm 18: 2, KJV; so *cast all your care upon him for he careth for you.* 1 Peter 5: 7, KJV

CHAPTER 9
HOW FAITH APPLIES TO OUR HEALTH

Faith is a discipline which is learned and developed through constant changes in your daily lives both spiritual and natural. It relates to obedience. The way in which you take care of your body is a statement that you are obedient to God. If you nurture your physical body there is no doubt that your spiritual 'body' won't be nurtured as well.

Food is a primary human need. When you eat you discipline the body to be receptive to nourishment. Being well nourished, the body becomes an effective instrument for spiritual maturation and transformation. Being selective in the kinds and types of foods and liquids you consume as well as the amount is very important to the body's function. Try to keep away from things that stress and harm the body. Whatever you do, you do unto God. So whatever you eat, you eat unto God. What you do unto the body, you do unto God.

You were created and made in His image and likeness.[32] Remember that your body is the temple of God. You should not for the sake of food and lavish living, destroy the work of God. Leviticus chapter 11 highlights a list of things which you should avoid eating. Why, because they are not healthy for the body. These creatures, no matter what they may eventually be transformed into unto your plate, clean up toxic waste, whether on land or in the water where there habitat is. These toxins that they ingest, remains in there system even after cooking and is transferred to the human system when consumed. Just imagine what these toxins do to your system after constantly eating these delicacies as they are called. Think about this!

People will argue that this particular chapter in the Bible is referring to religion. But if you look closer you will see the health aspect which is interrelated to the spiritual aspect of this chapter. One should therefore eat to be an instrument of God's will and purpose. People should eat to live and not live to eat.

As already established, faith is one of nine aspects comprising the Fruit of the Spirit. The interrelationship with faith and its other eight counterparts does affect your health. Longsuffering which I will refer to as patience is purity which when practiced can prevent illness and or dis-ease in your body. You are able to accept things and or events that you are unable to control. When you wait calmly before making rash hasty decisions, you are able to think and make a connection with others at different levels. Therefore forming a relationship that otherwise would not be. This helps to strengthen your emotions and spiritual awareness. With all this positiveness in you, there is no room for anxiety and frustration which is at the root of stress and we all know that stress contributes to multiple illness. In a nut shell stress KILLS.

CHAPTER 10
TAKE THE LIMITS OFF!

Where man is limited, it is an opportunity for God to bless him. Faith is not based on emotions. It is not about how "I" feel at a particular moment. For example, when God spoke to Sara and told her she was going to bare a child, her response was based on how she felt. She was past childbearing age, so she thought God was probably mistaking her for someone else. This is what happened to Sara, out went faith and in jumped feelings. I refer to the words spoken by Jesus in Matthew 15:8 & 9[33]. Some people believe that there is a God. They perform the 'rituals' of honoring God with their lips and not with their heart, it is for a show. They have not the faith that God can heal their cancer, aids, whatever affliction they suffer, deliver them from their grave situations etc. They have faith in man so they push aside the One who gave man the wisdom and understanding to do their jobs. Some people pray but have no patience. They are double-minded and therefore unstable in their thinking as James puts it in chapter1 verse 8. If the truth be told, some prayers for healing and deliverance are actually for relief. Drive-through service is what is requested. I put in my prayer, receive instant relief and away I go. I can't wait for tomorrow, a week, a month, six months you name it, to get my healing or deliverance. I need it now. You see God does not operate like we want him to. He is a God of order.

There is a time and purpose for everything under the heaven.[34] Let us therefore pray, believe and leave it alone for God to do his work. Exercise the faith that cast out all doubts, that no matter how I feel, I know I am healed, delivered and set free. The Lord promised that whatever you ask for in his name and having faith, it is given unto you. Jesus referred to certain people in the Bible as having Great Faith. The Syrophoenician woman whose daughter was demon possessed (Matt 15:21), the Centurion whose servant was sick with palsy, who told Jesus to say the word and his servant shall be healed (Matt 8:5-13). To this list I will also add, the woman with the issue of blood, who had faith that if she touched Jesus' clothes the anointing would flow through to her body and heal her. My, my, my. Just thinking about it shows how full were these persons' faith tank. These people were not thinking of what I did in the past or how much money I spent for help. They were greatly in need of help and heard of a man who could help. They had faith and put aside pride, ignored embarrassment and shame and reached out to the Restorer for restoration in their lives. If you show great faith, God will bless you, even if the blessing was not initially intended for you.35 Faith means letting go of the past and step into the future. Don't sit in the "comfortable" hurt and pain but venture out into the great unknown. The story of the four lepers showed presumptuous faith. They refused to let the Social standards eliminate them from their blessings. They put aside their afflictions and decided if we die, we die but we are not staying here and limit ourselves.36 Metaphorically speaking, the lepers in this scenario represent God's chosen who are set apart from the society because of their disposition; and God's authority to uproot the disobedient so His chosen can inherit the heritage of the heathen.

Paul said he had to let go of the things that were in his past so he could look forward towards his future which is the mark of the higher calling. Sometimes you are "comfortable" with your status in life and with the little that you have, that you miss the vision that lies ahead. You have to learn to unlearn some of the things you have learnt so you can learn what God wants you to learn. The greatness waiting ahead in the unknown will not be realized until you have great faith and step out into the "deep". Luke relates a story how Jesus taught his disciples to leave their comfort zone and step out in faith to receive greatness.[37]

Someone might say my faith is weak and tend to give up before a result is received. Your faith is not weak. Faith is faith. It's neither weak nor strong. Paul stated in Romans 12:3 that, God gives to every man a measure of faith. He does not give to some strong faith and some weak faith. He gives you faith and it is up to you to activate that faith to the level where you can receive optimum results. For example, when your automobile has ¼ tank of petrol does the strength (grade) of the petrol decreases? Or does the strength increases when the tank is full? What happens is that with a ¼ tank you get less mileage as oppose to a full tank. The strength of the petrol still remains the same whether ¼, ½ or full tank. So it is with your faith, it is the level at which your faith reaches that makes the difference on the volume of the return that you will receive.

Your expectation(s) are limited. You can not see beyond your immediate perception. You have placed your expectation(s) in a 'box' and therefore the tendency is to control the situation as well as the result. The 'box' now becomes an impediment and thwart the process. So the expected result can not happen, because there are limitations. Your viewpoint of the situation needs to be changed. There are limits which you did not perceive or calculate beforehand. Then frustration kicks in and you want to give up. You have accepted your limitations as the norm of your existence. Therefore you expect certain things to happen for you. However you can change your low expectations, so you can accomplish greater miracles in your life. You have to change your way of thinking.

CHAPTER 11
LACK OF FAITH EQUALS SIN

Whatever does not proceed from faith is sin. The apostle Paul highlighted the fact that when there is doubt there is no faith. Where there is no faith there is sin.[38] Peter also made mention of this in Luke 5:8 when he fell at Jesus' feet and prayed that he was not worthy to be around Jesus because of his sinful state. He could not contain himself when he witnessed the miracle catch.

David's lack of faith in God to fight the battle and not focus on man power caused him much loss of is army as well as pain and torment.[39] David wanted to show off how strong his army was so he listened to Satan and ordered a census. He was relying on the strength and power of his men instead of the power of God to deliver them from the hands of the enemy. David's reason for the census was wrong. He forgot that his real strength came from God and not from man. David was puffed up with selfish pride which was instigated by Satan. I guess he forgot that the wages of sin is death.

Why does your faith waver? Because, you have removed the focus from your destination or goal, and placed it on your present state on the journey. Peter only started to sink when his focus was taken from Jesus and was placed on himself.

Chapter 12
Don't' weigh my future against my present weight

The Bible tells us, that mankind form opinions of his peers future, based on their present appearance.[40] They believe only what the natural eyes sees. That is absolutely wrong, but when you pass judgment on yourself, that his absolutely Faithless.

Depicted in the Bible is a story about Hannah's inability to have children. Her enemy would provoke her because of her barrenness (1Samuel 1:1-28). She became frustrated and heartbroken and was reduced to tears and stopped eating. Her husband didn't mind the fact she was barren, because he loved her more than his other wife. He would give Hannah double portion when he gave the other wife and children less on the day that he offered sacrifices to God on his yearly visit to the temple. When her husband saw how depressed she was, he tried to cheer her up, by telling her not to worry. He told her that he is better to her than 10 sons. Despite her husband's support, she was not satisfied with her present situation. She knew she was missing something. She interceded with God and made a covenant with him that if he (God) would bless her womb with a male child, she would offer the child back to Him to be used in the temple. God agreed to the covenant. She conceived and bore a son whose name was Samuel.

Penniah (Hannah's adversary) is an example of the "judgmental world" that "writes you off" because of your present situation. Situation(s) cause by circumstances beyond your control. People will watch you and mark you as a target. But if you heed the words of the Prophet Isaiah (chapter 54:1-3), then no matter what people say about you, it will not bother you one bit. When the adversaries and the critics come against you just take it to the Lord in prayer. Sometimes those closest to you may not understand your actions and misjudge you. Some people's relationship with God is not at the level you are at. They will not recognize what you are doing and you might have made them aware of the attitude and actions of a True Believer. So don't judge me when you don't understand my actions. (Because) It is to God that I say my innermost secrets and when I commune with him I might look weird to you. But God understands just right. So label and judge me as much as you want today, because I will just keep praying and tomorrow dawns a new day. As the Prophet Isaiah assures me to "arise and shine for my light as come and the glory of the Lord is risen upon me...." [41]

Chapter 13
Looking through the eyes of God

If you can not see yourself as God sees you, you will not be able to walk in your greatness. From reading the stories of Ruth and Esther, one can conclude that these women saw themselves through faith, the way in which God saw them. They had separate lives but had so much in common. They had humble beginnings.

Ruth was a Moabitess before she married Naomi's son. When she became a widow and her mother-in-law wanted for her to go and find another (husband) life, she decided I am not going anywhere without you. I am going to take care of you. You have no one to take care of you so I am not leaving you. In those days widows were neglected and not looked after. She being a widow herself (but was a lot younger than her mother-in-law) was selfless in actions and displayed loyalty to Naomi. She knew that if she followed Naomi and took care of her, God will make a way out for them. And so he did.

Ruth had no right in Boaz's field but she was favored by God. Ruth knew that God had some thing in store for her. She became the wife of the rich man Boaz. So she as well as Naomi was taken care of for the rest of their lives. God rewarded Ruth for her faithfulness to Naomi in the lowest time of Naomi's life. She not only lost her husband but both sons as well.[42]

Haddasah[43] was a pretty orphan who was raised by her cousin. Like Ruth, she had no right to be in the King's court. But cousin Mordecai saw her has God saw her; as Queen Esther. She was meek and humble in spirit. She did not match up to the other candidates. But God's favor was on Esther. He allowed Hegai the king's Chamberlain to favor Esther. Therefore Hegai did for her what he did not do for the other maidens. He saw that Esther was special. She was transformed from orphan Esther to Queen Esther when she was chosen by the king. She became the vessel that God wanted to use to help bring about change to the Jewish people at that time.[44]

Jephthah was the son of a prostitute and Gilead (who had other sons with his wife). He was considered a bastard. He was denied right to his father's possession by his half brothers who chased him out of the country. He did nothing to receive such treatment from his brothers. After he was exiled Jepthah settled in the land of Tob were he became a mighty man of bravery with many warriors under is control. Despite the crude treatment which was mete out to him he allowed God to control him. Little did his brothers know that the stone that the builder refused would become the head corner stone. Trouble hit home to Israel, they were under attack from the Ammonites. Jephthah was sent for by the leaders of the land from where he was first exiled. He was sent away as a bastard but was brought back as the ruler over the inhabitants of Gilead and as commander of the army. God worked powerfully in Jephthah's life. He was a man of wisdom who tried to solve the situation peacefully. Jephthah judged Israel with God as his true judge for six years after which he died.[45]

After you have suffered for a season, God will establish you and elevate you. Faith is hearing the word and believing that God has an expected end for your life.

CHAPTER 14
...LIKE A MUSTARD SEED....

Have you ever felt empty, heartbroken, nothing you do has significance? You feel like you are at the end of your rope and feel like giving up on life? You think that the way to escape the pain, lack and hurt is to kill yourself. You thought you tried every thing possible, but one person you have not tried and he is Jesus. Peter invites you to cast all your cares upon Him for he cares for you.[46] Jesus is your last straw from destruction.

Someone once said a drowning man will clutch at a straw. Can the straw save him? Literally, no but he has confidence that somehow the straw will be his savior. His natural eyes see the straw but his expectation is way beyond that which his vision picks up. What that straw represents at that moment in time, is a huge log on which he can float to reach the security of stable ground. He is not critical of the size of the object in sight, but the fact that there is hope for him to get out of his predicament. He will 'clutch for dear life' to the object because he needs to be saved from the present situation. Jesus once told his disciples that if they had faith like a mustard seed, they can do miraculous things.[47]

Remember David, the little shepherd boy and Goliath the giant. David's protection from Goliath was only a sling and small stone. David was confident that the little stone and sling would help him to be victorious over Goliath. The stone was his faith and the sling was God's mercy and together they displaced the mighty Goliath from his place of power.[48]

Daniel when cast into the lions den did not waver but continued to pray believing that God will deliver him from being the lions dinner. He was not afraid to publicly acknowledge and worship God. Therefore God sent angels to protect Daniel, by preventing the lions from opening their mouths.[49]

Hananiah, Azariah and Mishael were three Jewish boys who along with Daniel were favored by the king. These three men refused to deny their God by bowing to the King. So they were bound hands and feet and cast into the fiery furnace. These men had great faith. Picture this, your feet and hands bound and you're thrown into a fiery furnace. You are charred remains before you even get burned. And your only means of escape is to deny the God of heaven and bow to the king. What would you do? These men did not second guess, nor were they doubled-minded but anchored their faith in God. Their attitude was, if we die we die, but no way are we going to worship man and deny God.[50]

CHAPTER 15
SMALL THINGS PRODUCES GREAT RESULTS

"...yet the dogs eat the crumbs from the Master's table." This was the Gentile woman's response to Jesus when he stalled her blessing. The dogs realizes that the crumbs, insignificant as they appear, are just as powerful as the whole bread. The crumbs can fill the hunger that lurks within you, executing the same action that the whole bread can perform. The crumbs, as small as they are, can give great satisfaction and peace. This mother realized that she was out of place seeking something that was intended for someone other than herself. However she did not give up, but understood that she had to change her attitude, her way of thinking to receive the blessing that was meant for others. So she decided, 'I will settle for the crumbs (the little, the vague, the insignificant) and find my rightful place with my Savior.' She did not need money to receive her blessing all she needed was, to have faith in God. (Luke tells a story where Lazarus, being destitute and covered with sores, yearned for the crumbs that fell from the rich man's table to satisfy his hunger.)[51]

The woman with the issue of blood held on to the hem of Jesus' clothes and received what many doctors could not give. She probably spent all her money, even sold assets to procure financial resource to pay for help for her condition. Nothing worked for over 12 years. But one insignificant idea she had out of desperation and put into action by her Faith and having the right attitude, produced significant results. NO MONEY WAS NEEDED.

Two fishes and five loaves fed 5000 plus, with ample leftovers. NO MONEY was spent to feed this multitude of hungry people. But Jesus' Faith and his faith in His Father, was able to multiply the small lunch to feed the people. Our blessing is tied up in our faith or lack of faith there of.

God created mankind from the dust of the earth. NO MONEY was needed to put God's Master-plan into action. He is Faith itself and all he had to do was speak it. So he created man in the spirit first and foremost and then in the natural.[52] He used the simple, insignificant thing as the dust, to bring man into existence.

There was a man who was born crippled and each day he was carried and laid at the gate of the temple, Beautiful. His condition prevented him from earning a livelihood, so he had to beg passers- by in order to support himself. So when he saw Peter and John coming his way he did what he had the physical ability to do - stretch out his hands begging. He expected to get something no matter how small it was, when Peter said to him "look at us". So his attention was focused on Peter and John. Imagine how he must have felt when he heard the words "Silver and Gold I have none." Peter continued talking "but that which I have I give to you." At this point the man realized he would not get money from these two men but that he would receive something. Then Peter said "in the name of Jesus Christ of Nazareth rise up and walk."[53] NO MONEY was needed for this man's healing. He thought that money was the answer to his situation. The answer to his problem was to have faith in God Almighty, for the restoration of the life that was intended for him by God.

Like this man, many people think that if they have money they can do whatever they want. They can live the life they dream of. But a lot of people who are wealthy have said that they have all the financial resource that they could need but lack true happiness. Why? Because they lack one thing. That is, Faith in Jesus Christ. Money cannot buy peace of mind. It cannot buy happiness. What it is used for is to buy things that people perceive will make them happy. Hebrews 11:1 AMP. assures you that Faith is the confirmation, the title/ deed of the things you hope for in life. It is the validation of things you are unable to see with the physical eyes. It is the strong belief of the reality that is not made known to the senses.

CHAPTER 16
KEYS TO UNLOCK FAITH

The devil causes your spirit to be locked into a particular thing, which limits your spiritual vision. But you can unlock it and tap into the unknown, unidentified greatness of God, by removing the barriers that holds your Faith. The ability to unlock your Faith is dependent on how much focus you place on God. There are few things which you need to do. I will refer to them as keys to unlock the door that prevents your faith from being completely released.

1. Prayer.

One of the keys to release Faith is to connect your belief with prayer. Prayer is the key to survival. Pray earnestly and wait upon God to do his work.[54] This increases your ability to perceive tangibility and releases the inclination to put thoughts and words into action. Call unto Him and he will show thee great and mighty things which you know not of.[55] Pray without ceasing.[56] There is a coined phrase that tells you to **PUSH; P**ray **U**ntil **S**omething **H**appens. When you **PRAY** you must give praise unto God, as **P**raises **R**eleases **A**uthority to **Y**ou.

Pray the prayer of Faith like Jabez. The Bible depicts Jabez as a man with much honor and compared to his brothers, he was very different. When Jabez's mother was giving birth to him she experienced a painful birth, one that she had never experienced before. So she decided to name this child to remind her of the pain and sorrow that she withstood during this birth.[57] Jabez grew to be a man whose life was nothing but grief, pain and sorrow. One day he decided,

"I have had enough of the cursed life and I am going to cash in on my faith in God, now! So he prayed the Prayer of Faith. Let my life no longer be painful and fill with hardship. Remove the cup of grief that I have been force to drink from, all these years. Extend my borders and remove the markers that have kept me in a box. Remove the limitations that have prevented me from moving ahead. No more will my life be framed by negativity. No longer will I accept this situation. I want out NOW! I need your protection Lord, that the evil of my past will not be a plague to me. And God granted his petition.

2. Meditation.

Meditate on the Word of God constantly.[58] Concentrate with real focus. This means involving the senses to be apart of such activity which will produce remarkable results. You will realize a higher level of perception and awareness in God. The mind 'tunes out' many things around you occasionally, but if you really pay attention you'll be amazed to know what you are missing. Train your 'mind' to tune out the negative and tune into the spirit realm.

David (a man of meditation) expressed how he loves to meditate on the Lord's commandments and he does it continuously throughout the day. He implies that he was helpless without the Word of God. He expressed this in Psalms119:97,105 where he said that God's Word is a lamp unto his feet and a light unto his path.

The Lord appeared unto Joshua after the death of Moses and expressed that the book of the law should not depart from his (Joshua's) mouth.[59] He emphasized the importance of meditating on the word of God to lead him to prosperity and success.

3. Remove the limits off God.

Change your expectations of the results by taking the limits off God. You have to be specific in your asking but you should not dictate the results. Let God have his way. Understand that the result might not come in the 'packaged form' that you have perceived. However the result that you receive is the ideal response that God willed for life.[60]

4. Take Action

Faith without works is dead.[61] There is no two way about that. For example, you go to work with the expectation that at the end of the work week you will receive compensation. You had faith to get the job, but now that you got the job, to get money you have to show up and work for it. Work without Faith is lacking common sense. Picture yourself going to work and when the paycheck is given to you, you say "oh no, I don't want money, I just like to work." They will probably think you're from outer space. So when you go to God asking for something you must understand that some action on your part is involved. As in the natural, so in the Spiritual. The Spiritual world works similarly to the natural world. Here is a formula you can always keep in mind. **Faith is: Action (work) + Belief (expectation) = Blessing (success).** Solomon said in Proverbs 16:3, to commit your works unto the Lord and thy thoughts or desires will be established.

If you practice using these keys on a daily basis, you too can be like the Holy men and women who are highlighted in the Bible. You can experience and accomplish great miracles and wonders.

CHAPTER 17
WHEN GOD SAYS NO!

Have you ever asked God for something and you think he says no? What do you do then after the request is not granted? God is your Father and your source and if he refuses, where do you go? The scripture says that I don't receive of God because I don't ask.[62] Yet when I ask I don't receive. Here goes, there is a response when you think that God does not respond to you. You have to assess your attitude as well as your character to find out why you were denied. If you applied for a loan and was denied you will want to know the reason(s) you were refused. Then you will try to work around the shortcomings and reapply. The same principles work with God. There is a yes in God's no. When the Lord says no to you it is either of two things.

(1) Your request is out of order.

God knows what is in your best interest. Your Faith in him allows you to say, "Lord you know what is best for me, so let thy will be done. I am not going to be upset because every disappointment for me is an appointment with you." 'Flesh' may sometimes get in the way and we ask selfishly. Lust sometimes leads you to attempt certain task, without referring to God first, to ask if it is his will for you. Then you get stuck and that's when you call upon him and expect him to say yes and run to your rescue. God is a jealous God and he requires that you put nothing or no one before him. You should never use him as a last resort. Remember David, how he did the ungodly act of setting up Uriah to be killed to get Bathseba to be his wife? God allowed David to have his fun (time,) but when Bathsheba gave birth to David's seed, God cursed the seed (2 Samuel 11 and 12).

(2) The timing is not right.

God knows everything as well as he sees everything and everyone. He is omnipotent, omniscient and ever-present. God told Jeremiah[63] that he knew him long before he God created him into being. God made a blue print of the life of everyone. He knows exactly the number of hair strands you have on your head, for those who do have. You have limited vision and therefore you cannot see what is ahead of you unless he tells you. So he tells you to wait, by not responding to your request. Take for instance the story of Lazarus, Mary and Martha in John 11:1-45. Lazarus became sick so his sisters sent for Jesus. Jesus did not respond to their request. He waited two days before he decided to go see Lazarus. Then Lazarus died and the message of his death was told to Jesus. Note carefully as the scripture states, that Jesus loved Lazarus as well as Mary and Martha. It was not that he did not care about them. The miracle which was predestined could not happen without the death of Lazarus. So he (Jesus) could not go before his time.

In Mark 11:12-14, 20-26 Jesus demonstrated the importance of timing to his disciples. At first glance, your assumption was that because Jesus was hungry and could not get any fig to eat from the tree he became angry and cursed the tree. Go to verses 20 through 26 and you will realize that Jesus could command the tree to bear fruit so he could eat. He did not. Why? Because the lesson was not about eating it was about the right timing. Seed, Time and Harvest. This is clearly expressed in Ecclesiastes 3:1-8. It is very important that things are done in a timely fashion. Otherwise you can become frustrated and or angered and your reaction can affect you as well as others.

When God keeps you waiting it is that there is a greater good in the blessing he has scheduled for you; but because some persons who should be apart of the blessing are not in their right position as yet, he has to play the waiting game with you. So you think he ignores you. You see, more people will benefit from his response to you on his timing than you alone, if he answers when you want him to. People's life will change immensely and God will be glorified. This why longsuffering is an attribute of the Fruit of the Spirit. When you are long suffering, you will wait patiently on God for his response.

God is able to prevent you from falling prey to the enemy when you request help, not knowing what negativity surrounds the things you requested. He delays his response and then you think he denies your request. Delay does not mean denial. It means that God is waiting for the opportune moment to bless you. Always remember that first and foremost, God **must** receive glory from your request. If not then your request is selfish.

CHAPTER 18
THE PROCESS

There is an old chorus that I learnt when I was a child and constantly heard my grandmother sang on a regular basis. It was "spirit-lifter" so to speak and it goes like this:

Some through the water
Some through the flood
Some through the fire
But all through the blood
Some through great sorrow
But God gave a song
In the night season
And all the day long.

Now that I am older I realize that folks like my grandmother and other ancestors had faith in God so when faced with adversity they found comfort in singing songs that reinforce their Faith in God. They never gave up despite the treatment that they received from the hands of the adversary and what life had to offer. This reminds me of a time in my adult years, when I decided to get back on track with God. I was on "fire" for the Lord but I had to undergo a process of change to go to the next level in Christ. It was a rough, rough time, being a single mother with a teenage daughter and had lost every reasonable source of income. I remember that at one instance when I became frustrated and the Lord spoke to me and said "don't fan the flame, let the fire burn". I was obedient because at this point in my walk with God I had already received reassurance from God about different situations. So I knew what he wanted for me to do, to be patient and let him take me through the process and having faith in him I will come out like fine gold.

God allows things to happen to you for valid reasons. You will become stronger in your walk with him, your faith level increases and he will get the glory. Don't look at your circumstance and attack the devil. The devil has no power. He can do nothing to harm you without permission from God or from you. You have everything to gain from Satan's temptations. Paul reassures you that the trying of your faith only makes you stronger in God. Just remember Job's story how he received double for his troubles and God received the glory.

When Jesus was about to be crucified he went through various trials. God allow the trials, mocking, spitting, scorning, scourging, everything that was negatively directed at Jesus for the greater good. He knew that at the end of it all that Jesus would defeat death and be transformed from the earthly body to the heavenly body. He would become more powerful and mightier, in the form of the Holy Ghost. At the end of life's trials and tribulation' you will enjoy the thrill of victory and Satan will have to suffer the agony of defeat.

The scripture reads,[64] "choose whom you will serve this day". The crucifixion of Jesus depicted how he was mocked and jeered at by his killers saying "Hail King of the Jews". I feel that there were some onlookers who thought that Jesus was in fact the King of the Jews and hated the brutal treatment which was dished out to him. But they feared for their lives so instead of separating themselves and standing up they remain hidden in the crowd. Remember Peter?[65] Their faith tank had run out and they became cowards.

A true characteristic of Faith is the ability to separate yourself from the masses, who will 'drown' you. You are afraid to 'stand out', so therefore compromise your faith to fit in to the so-called 'functional society', a society that lacks morals and Christ-like values. When God wanted to use Abram He gave him a new name which is Abraham.[66] Then He told him to separate himself from his relatives. Abraham did not fully understand what separation meant so he went ahead and took his nephew Lot with him. This decision later caused grievance between them. It was only after he parted company with Lot, did the prosperity that God had promised him started to manifest.[67] **See illustration below.**

Obedience vs disobedience in relation to separation

Obedience ↔ separation from the world ↔ deliverance → blessing & favor (wages)

↑

Disobedience → separation → → repentance → → ↑

(from God)

↓

refuse to repent

↓

↓

destruction (wages)

Another example is found in Isaiah chapter 6 where the prophet said, "In the year King Uzziah died I saw also the Lord sitting upon a throne, high and lifted up, and his train filled the temple...." What happen to Isaiah here? His spiritual vision was blocked by his attention towards the earthly king. However, when the king died, the veil was lifted and Isaiah was able to receive commission from God.

Moses disassociated himself from Pharoah and his kingdom. He did not want to be known as the son of Pharoah's daughter. Why? Because he knew that God had chosen him for something special. Therefore he could not be faithful to God and Pharoah at the same time. He had to choose who he was faithful to. Moses was foreordained to be elevated by God. If you haven't read the story of Moses, one would say that Moses was ungrateful. He turned against the one who raised him from a child to a man. The reality is that Moses was a "silent" enemy of Pharoah, whom he (Pharoah) set out to kill at an infant stage. Pharoah suffered from insecurity. Little did he know that the child he was a "grandfather" to was in-fact the one he wanted to murder. The one he was fearful of, eventually taking away his kingdom. God's favor on Moses allowed Pharoah to foster and train his own rival. Pharoah thought that he was wise by trying kill the child before he became a man to challenge him, but in Romans 1: 22 Paul spoke of ...professing themselves to be wise, they became fools. And that was Pharoah.

CHAPTER 19
DARE TO BE DIFFERENT

Here I refer to the woman who had the issue of blood for 12 years. This woman was in a sense a "shut out" or as was commonly known then as unclean. She would not be allowed to go near the Master. Knowing her limitations in society as well as her need to be in contact with Jesus, she could not approach the situation as others did. She could not go directly to Jesus because of fear of being cast aside. So she must have given a lot of thought about her present situation; the limitation of being a shut-out and the limitation that her dis-ease brought about. She did not know how to get Jesus' attention without the crowd noticing her. Frustrated she said to herself, "if I can just find a way to touch the hem of Jesus' clothes, I know I will be healed". She was passionate about needing a miracle in her life today, so she could not give up. She knew she had to be different in her approach. Hence her healing was not like other miracles. No one before had ever touch Jesus' clothes and was healed.

One woman's faith and perseverance started an all-important action in the Healing Ministry which is still proficient today in the Christian Faith. The belief is that a piece of cloth when prayed over and anointed by an ordained, anointed person, along with the individual(s) faith in God for their healing, then supernatural healing can occur. It is recognized as a point of contact to God along with their prayers. Like this woman, each person's ministry is significant and unique. But many times people want similar ministerial anointing as others. Until we lose this mind-set of wanting to be an imitator or a copycat, then your anointing as well as your blessing will be tied up and will not be release. Because what you are telling God indirectly is that you don't want what he has for you. You want what so and so have. You like to be like the "Joneses". Brothers and sisters, dare to be different. Who knows, many, many years to come that you won't be one of the many people in history whose story will be highlighted over and over and over.

CHAPTER 20
HAVING THE RIGHT ATTITUDE

Your attitude after being blessed is equally important as your attitude before you receive your blessing. It is easier to loose something than to gain it. Scriptural references Matthew 23:12 and Luke 14 :11 brings to focus the words of Jesus while, he was on earth, that if you become selfishly proud you will be brought low. Why? Because you have removed the focus from God to yourself. You have now become carnal in your thinking and action. You have Eased God Out. Paul spoke of having plenty to boast about and would be no fool (not lying) in doing so because he would be telling the truth.[68] But he refuses to do so because he does not want anyone to get the 'wrong message'; even though he has received wonderful revelations from God. To prevent Paul from become puffed up with selfish pride, God allows a messenger from Satan which he called "thorn in his flesh" to afflict him. He operated with humility towards God and therefore presented himself as a servant. Peter advises that you should be clothed with humility. For God resists the proud, and gives grace to the humble. Humble yourselves therefore under the mighty hand of God, that he may exalt you in due time.[69]

Chapter 21
Reap the Rewards

God establishes you only when you are faithful to him. Here are some of the faithful few who received blessings because of their obedience to God.

Abraham being the friend of God, became the father of many nations. He was blessed in earthly possession as well.

Jehosaphat was established by God as King of Judah and all the people of Judah brought him presents. He was highly favored and he had riches and honor in abundance. He was victories in many military battles.

Jephthah was controlled by the Spirit of God in all his endeavors. He became ruler and judge over his own people after he was exiled from his homeland by his brothers.

Esther the orphan became Queen and delivered her people from the destruction of Haman.

Solomon was known as the wisest man that ever lived. He was chosen by God, before he was born, to build a house for the Ark of God. He was faithful to God and fulfilled the purpose that God intended for him. Not only was he wise but he was wealthy has well.

Shiphrah and Puah were mid-wives who defied Pharoah's order to kill the infant males when they were born. God blessed them and the people multiplied and grew mighty (Exodus 1).

Rahab the harlot put her life and the life of her family in danger from the authorities that be, when she hid the spies in her house. She as well as her family were saved and spared from the plague.

Ruth was faithful and being a widow took care of her widowed mother-in-law. Her reward was that she became the wife of wealthy Boaz and became a part of the lineage of Jesus. She became apart of history.

CONCLUSION

Faithfulness to the work of God will 'move' God to release treasures unto you. He will let your enemies bless and honor you. He will overtake you with favor. That's what he did for Jehoshaphat in 2 Chronicles 17. After you have suffered for a season, God will establish you and lift you up.[70]

Blessings are available to all who are willing to sacrifice and be disciplined to the will of God. God does not choose certain people and bless them. It is one's decision to kill the flesh and extol the Spirit of God on a daily basis. Release your Faith! If you don't then you are your greatest enemy against your Faith.[71]

When you entrust your money in the care of a financial institution, you do so on the basis that they offer the best benefits to you, not better but the best. You have faith in them that your best interest is their priority. If your are so trusting in man, why can't you have faith in the One who gives the best of the best return on your deposit. All you have to deposit in God is your Faith and trust. Put away fear from you so you can receive from God that which you have requested. You see, happiness is not found in riches or possession or stuff. It is found in the inner peace which God gives to you. So you can enjoy the 'stuff' that you have required.[72]

You have to be confident and convincing that your petition is sincere. When you cast your cares upon God, then you can focus your attention on worshiping and thanking Him for the desired outcome. No longer are you frustrated and laden down with worries and concerns. You no longer expect failure, but exercise your faith and think positively. You are sober and vigilant and are able to wait upon God, despite any attack from the adversary.[73]

While God walked the earth in the form of his son, Jesus, he placed emphasis on the welfare of orphans, the poor, widows and the strangers. The social and spiritual welfare of these people should be an integral part of your daily life which enhances your daily walk with God. When you passionately and genuinely reach out to the needy, you touch the heart of God and therefore he blesses you. God has never been and will never be a debtor to any man. He will reward you for every work you do in his name.

Help thy brother's boat across and LO! thine own has reached the shore.[74] Charles Dudley Warner said "It is of the beautiful compensations of this life that no one can sincerely try to help another without helping himself".[75] Marsha Sinetar's quote "ultimately, it is through serving others that we become fully Human", sums up our purpose here on earth. Qualify your faith by living by God's principles and he will give you both earthly and spiritual things. Be passionate to the things of God, because passionate Faith releases Power.

References

(Endnotes)

Introduction

[1] Quote taken from Benny Hinn's faith plaque.

[2] Ecclesiates 3:1: To everything there is a season and a time to every purpose under the heaven.

[3] Quote taken from Budda.

[4] Jeremiah 38:5-13

[5] Ruth chapter1: 1-22, Ruth chapters 2, 3 and 4.

[6] Paramount Pictures, "Fire Works Picture" 2001, "Rat Race", Whoopi Goldberg

Chapter 1

[7] Jeremiah 1:5.

[8] Jeremiah 29:11.

Chapter 2

[9] Hebrews 11:6.

Chapter 3

[10] See Figure 1

[11] See Figure 2

[12] St. John 1:1, 14.

[13] Hebrews 12:2

Chapter 4

[14] 2 Timothy 1:7.
[15] Excerpt from Joshua Wolf Shenk's book, "Lincoln's Melancholy", www.beliefnet. com/story177/story_17744.html

Chapter 5

[16] Genesis chapters 37,39,40,41

[17] Genesis 45:5-28

[18] Mark 11:24.

[19] Isaiah 65:24.

Chapter 6

[20]Proverbs 18:21.

[21] James 3:8

[22] Psalm 94:9

Chapter 7

[23] St. Matthew 24:35, Mark 13:31, Isaiah 40:8, Isaiah 55:11

[24] St. Luke chapter one: Birth of Jesus foretold.

[25] Exodus chapters one and two: Moses birth.

[26] Genesis chapters six, seven and eight

[27] St. Matthew 8:5-13

[28]St. Matthew 15:21-28 & St. Mark 7:24-30

Chapter 8

[29] Hebrews chapter 11

[30] Romans 10:17

[31] Twentieth Century Fox, "Dream Works Pictures" 2001, "Cast Away", Tom Hanks.

Chapter 9

[32] Genesis 1:26-27;

Chapter 10

[33] St. Matthew 15:8-9 AMP. These people draw near with their mouths and honor me with their lips, but their hearts hold off and are away from me. Uselessly do they worship me, for they teach as doctrines, the commandments of men. See also Isaiah 29:13.

[34] Ecclesiastes 3:1

[35] Proverbs 13:22b

[36] 2 Kings 7:3-9 AMP.

[37] St. Luke 5:1-10

Chapter 11

[38] (a) Romans14:23 AMP. But the man who has doubts (misgivings, an uneasy conscience) about eating, and then eats [perhaps because of you], stands condemned[before God], because he is not true to his convictions and he does not act from faith. For whatever does not originate and proceed from faith is sin [whatever is done without a conviction of its approval by God is sinful].

(b)Titus 1:15-16 AMP. To the pure [in heart and conscience] all things are pure, but to the defiled and corrupt and unbelieving, nothing is pure; their very minds and consciences are defiled and polluted. They profess to know to know God [to recognize, perceive, and be acquainted with Him], but deny and disown and renounce Him by what they do; they are detestable and loathsome, unbelieving and disobedient and disloyal and rebellious and [they are] unfit and worthless for good work (deed or enterprise) of any kind.

[39]1 Chronicle 21:1-30

Chapter 12

[40] 1Samuel 16:7b

[41]Isaiah 60:1-6

Chapter 13

[42] See book of Ruth

[43] Hadassah was Esther's original Jewish name. She was named Esther to disguise her ethnicity.
[44] See the book of Esther.

[45] See Judges chapter 11.

Chapter 14

[46] 1Peter 5:7

[47] St. Matthew 17:20
[48] See 1 Samuel Chapter 17

[49] See Daniel chapter 6

[50] See Daniel chapter 3

Chapter 15

[51] St Luke 16:19-21 AMP.

[52] Genesis 1:26-27

[53] Acts 3:2-12

Chapter 16

[54] Psalm 34: 4 & 17

[55] Jeremiah 33:3

[56] 1Thessalonian 5:17

[57] 1Chronicles 4:9 AMP.

[58] Psalms1:2 AMP. But his delight and desire are in the law of the Lord and on His law (precepts, instructions, teachings of God) he habitually meditates (ponders and studies) by day and by night.

[59] Joshua 1:8

[60] Genesis 18:9-14 and St. Luke 1:30-37

[61]James2:20 & 26

Chapter 17

[62] James 4:2c and James 4:3a

[63] Jeremiah 1:5

Chapter 18

[64] Joshua 24:15

[65] St Mark 14:66-72

[66] Abraham's name change was the first step in his separation from his kin folks.

[67] Genesis chapters 12 and 13.

Chapter 20

[68] 2 Corinthians 12:6-7 NLT

[69] 1Peter 5:5-6

Conclusion

[70] Daniel 3:30

[71] 1Peter 5:7

[72] Ecclesiastes 5:9-20 [17-20]

[73] 1Peter 5:8

[74] Hindu Proverb

[75] Proverbs11:24-25 & Psalms 37:26

BIBLIOGRAPHY

1. King James Version (KJV)

2. The Amplied Bible (AMP)

3. New Living Translation (NLT)